Earthquakes

By Elizabeth Drummond

Library For All Ltd.

Earthquakes

First published 2021

Published by Library For All Ltd
Email: info@libraryforall.org
URL: libraryforall.org

This book was made possible by the generous support of the Education Cooperation Program and the following organisations.

Australian Aid

ChildFund Australia

PLAN INTERNATIONAL

AHP Disaster READY

Earthquakes
Drummond, Elizabeth
ISBN: 978-1-922550-17-0
SKU01567

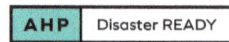

Earthquakes

Tectonic Plates

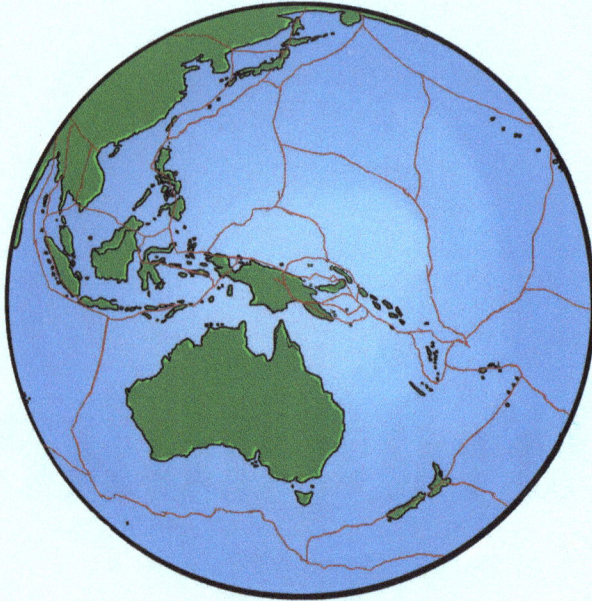

The surface of the Earth is not one single piece of land, but seven large pieces and lots of smaller ones that fit together like a jigsaw. These pieces are called tectonic plates.

The place where plates join together is called a fault line. Can you see it?

Tectonic plates move all the time. Usually they move very slowly and you don't feel anything. But sometimes the edge of the plate gets stuck while the rest of the plate keeps moving. When it finally breaks free and slams into a new position it causes the Earth to shake. This is called an earthquake.

Plates usually move about 2–5cm per year? This is as fast as your fingernails grow!

Did you know?

Tectonic plates move in three ways that can cause the ground to shake.

Convergent — one plate is forced over another. Many mountains have been formed this way.

Divergent — plates drift apart from each other. This can create new land or ocean floor.

Strike-slip — plates slide past each other.

DID YOU KNOW?

The New Guinea Highlands were formed by the collision of the Australian Tectonic Plate and the Pacific Plate. This is an example of convergence.

The ancient Japanese people believed earthquakes were caused by Namazu, a giant catfish that lived underground. When Namazu thrashed his tail he would cause violent earthquakes.

Many other peoples in the world also have explanations about what causes earthquakes. Perhaps there are stories in your own culture?

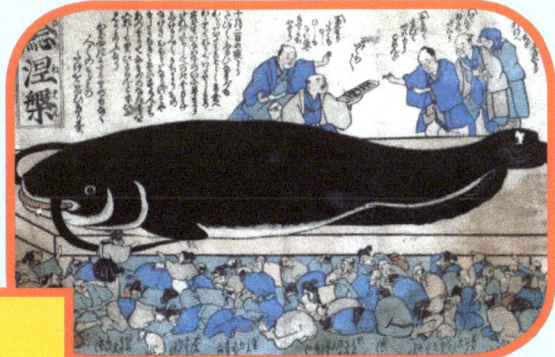

Namazu
the Earthshaker

Focus and epicentre

The place where the earthquake originates underground is called the focus. It can be deep below the Earth's surface.

The place on the Earth's surface directly above the focus is called the epicentre.

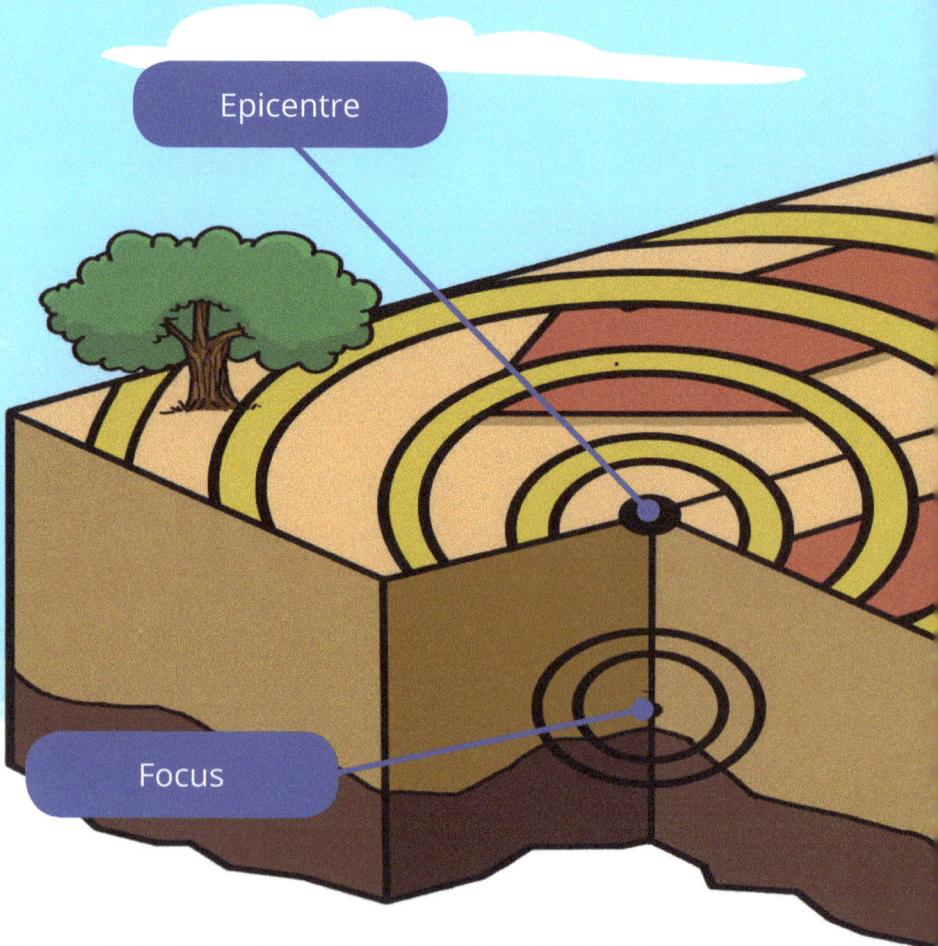

Epicentre

Focus

The energy released when plates bump or slide travels through the ground in the form of vibrations called seismic waves.

All of these factors interact when an earthquake occurs on the fault plane.

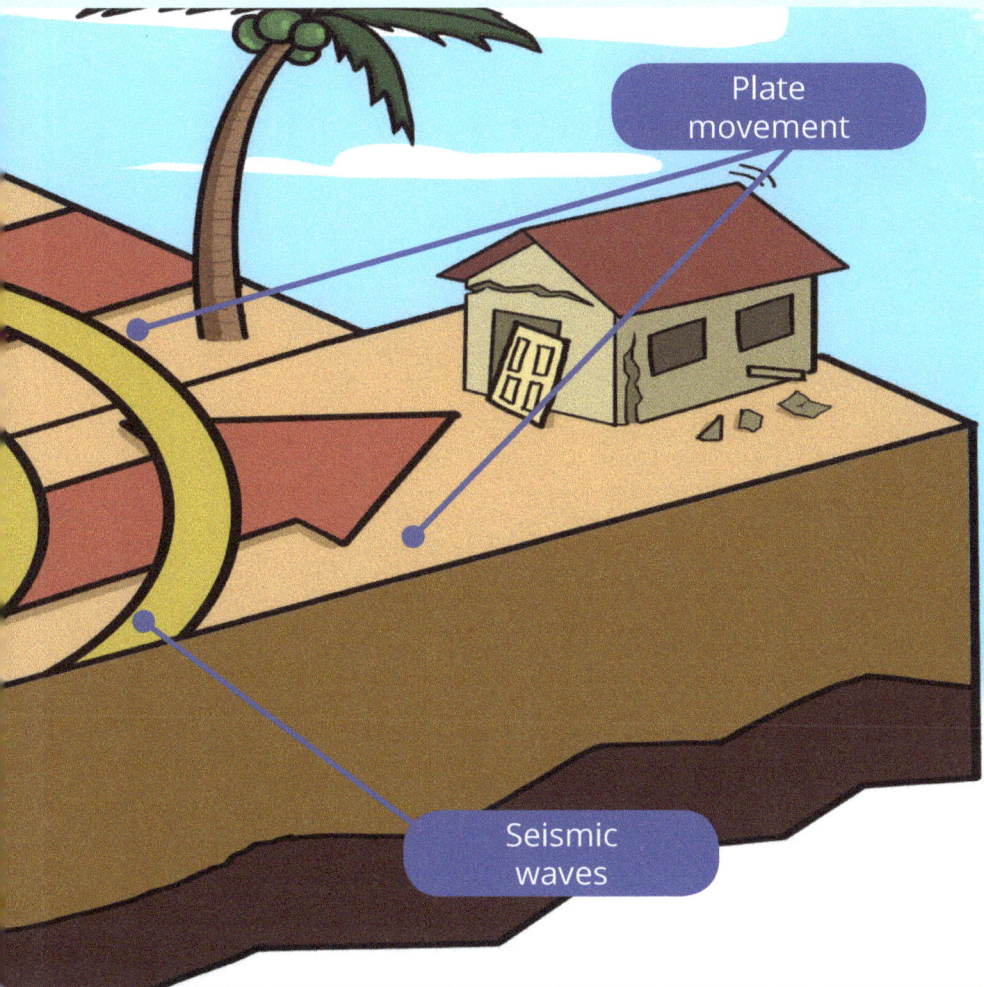

Plate movement

Seismic waves

DID YOU KNOW?

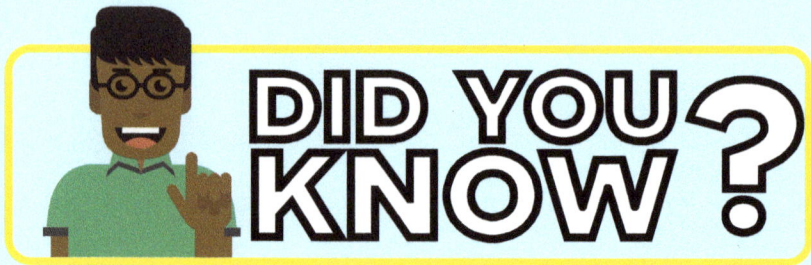

The ground usually shakes for about 10–30 seconds during an earthquake.

There are often smaller shakes before and after the main earthquake. These are called foreshocks and aftershocks.

Aftershocks can continue for weeks or even months after the main event.

How do you measure an earthquake?

The size of an earthquake depends on the size of the fault and the amount of slip. Scientists use a special instrument called a seismograph to measure how big an earthquake is.

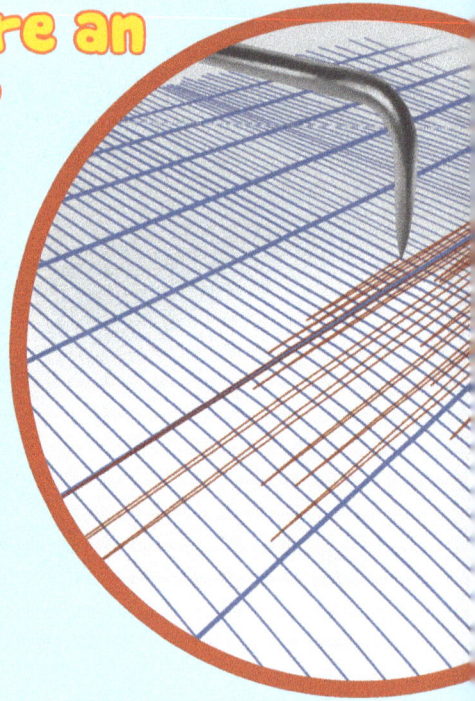

A small wiggly line means a small earthquake. A big wiggly line means a big earthquake.

The base is firmly attached to the ground.

Heavy weight hanging by a thread or spring with a pen attached to it.

Rotating drum with paper on it.

When the ground shakes the base moves but the hanging weight does not.

The difference between the shaking weight and the motionless heavy weight is recorded as the pen draws a line on the paper.

The Richter Scale

Earthquakes can be big or small. Scientists measure how big the earthquake is using a seismograph and give it a value on the Richter Scale of 1–8.

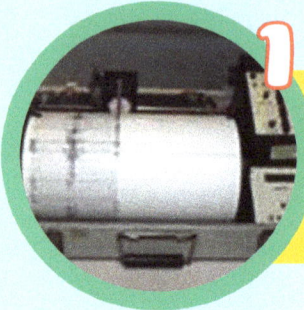

1 So small you won't feel anything.

2 Hanging objects sway.

3 Small vibrations that feel like a truck is driving by.

4 Small objects fall over and windows can break.

5 Furniture moves and chunks of plaster or wood can fall off walls.

6 Buildings are damaged.

7 Buildings fall over, the earth cracks, and underground pipes break.

8 Most buildings fall down and bridges are destroyed.

The earthquake with the biggest recorded magnitude was the Great Chilean Earthquake. It had a magnitude of 9.5 (approximately 9.5 on the Richter scale) and occurred in 1960. About 6000 people died because of the earthquake.

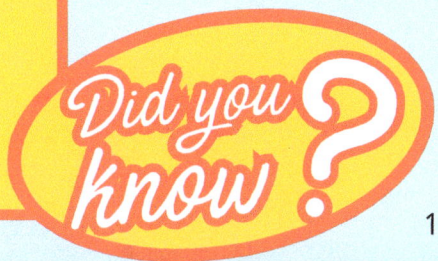

Did you know?

Tsunamis

Tsunami is a Japanese word for 'harbour wave.'
A tsunami can be caused by an earthquake that
occurs underwater.

An earthquake rocks the ocean floor.

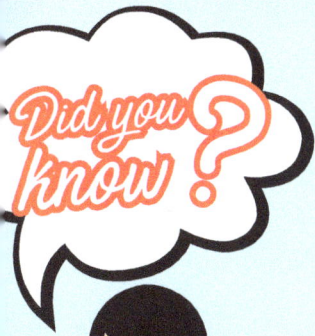

Some people believe that animals can sense when a tsunami is coming. This is probably because they have very good hearing and can sense vibrations caused by the tsunami before people can.

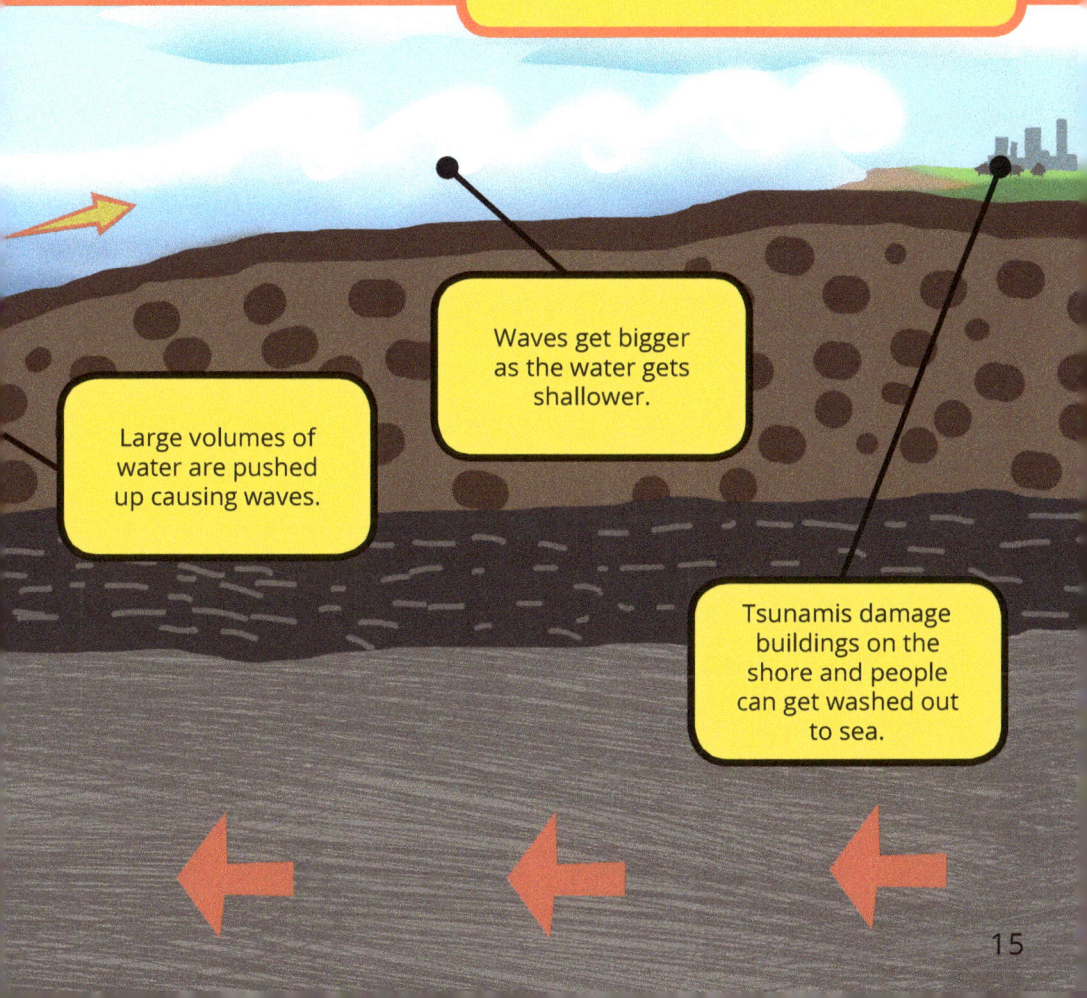

Waves get bigger as the water gets shallower.

Large volumes of water are pushed up causing waves.

Tsunamis damage buildings on the shore and people can get washed out to sea.

Stay safe INSIDE during an earthquake

1

Stay indoors until the shaking stops.

2

Take cover under a desk or table and hold on to it.

3

Stay away from windows and items that could fall on you.

17

Stay safe OUTSIDE during an earthquake

1

Move away from trees or buildings that can fall on you.

2

Find a flat area away from mountains in case the earth begins to slide down to the ground.

3

If you are near the beach, run away from the water's edge and move quickly to higher ground.

4

Stop driving if you are in a car and stay inside.

5

Once the shaking stops don't go inside until an adult has checked it is safe.

Be prepared!

Talk to your community about where it would be safe to go during an earthquake or a tsunami.

Work with your community to create an action plan.

20

Think about what you would take with you if you had to leave your house for a while.

It's Exam Time

Q What is the place where plates join called?
A A fault line.

Q How far do plates move per year?
A 2-5cm.

Q Who is Namazu the Earthshaker?
A A mythical giant catfish.

Q What is the focus of an earthquake?
A The underground location of the earthquake's origin.

Q How long does an earthquake usually last?
A 10-30 seconds.

Q What is an aftershock?
A A small shock that happens after the main quake.

Q How do scientists measure an earthquake?
A They use a seismograph.

Q What should YOU do to stay safe in an earthquake?
A Read this book again now!

It's time to prepare for an emergency!

Use your finger to trace the lines. Which items should go into the emergency kit? Which ones should stay at home?

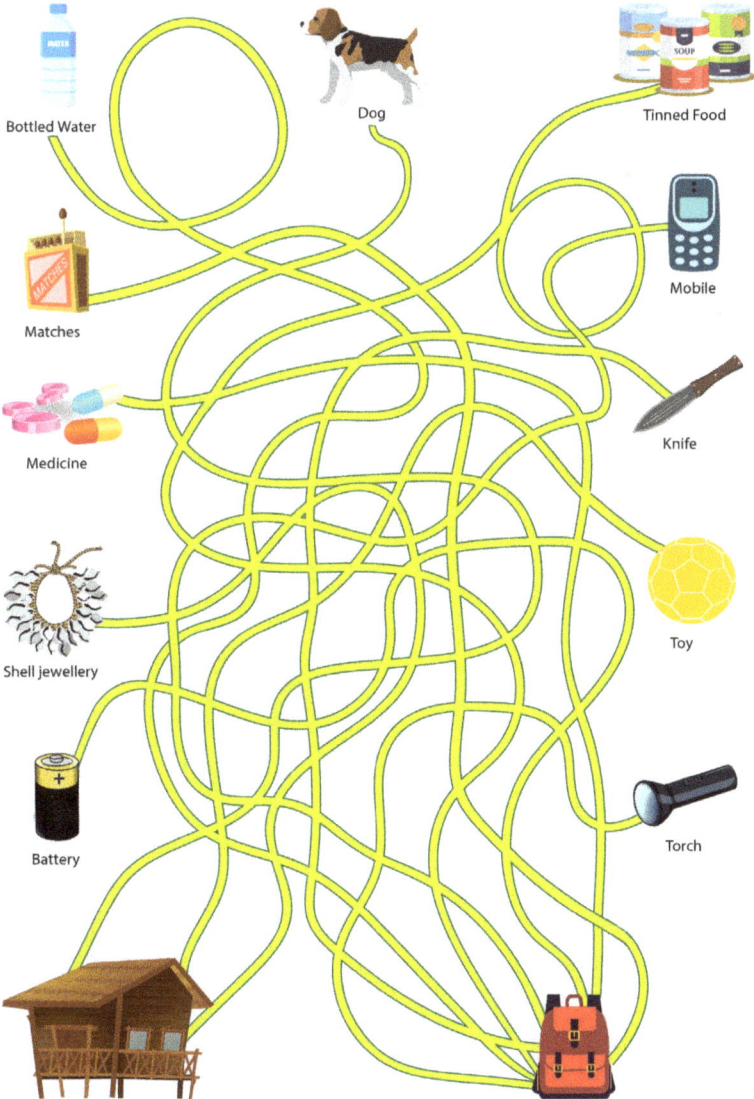

Bottled Water

Dog

Tinned Food

Matches

Mobile

Medicine

Knife

Shell jewellery

Toy

Battery

Torch

Photo credits

Page	Link
Cover	https://pixabay.com/photos/earthquake-rubble-collapse-disaster-1665878/
Title Cover	https://pixabay.com/photos/earthquake-fracture-asphalt-split-1665892/
5	https://en.wikipedia.org/wiki/Fault_(geology)#/media/File:Fault_in_Seppap_Gorge_Morocco.jpg
6-7	https://en.wikipedia.org/wiki/Plate_tectonics http://historyofgeology.fieldofscience.com/2011/01/namazu-earthshaker.html
11	https://pixabay.com/photos/earthquake-rubble-collapse-disaster-1665886/ https://commons.wikimedia.org/wiki/Earthquake#/media/File:Chuetsu_earthquake-earthquake_liquefaction1.jpg
12-13	https://www.vectorstock.com/royalty-free-vector/a-seismograph-vector-1854800
14-15	https://commons.wikimedia.org/wiki/File:Kinemetrics_seismograph.jpg https://pixabay.com/photos/lamp-lightbulb-electricity-old-1031516/ https://pixabay.com/photos/semi-trailers-truck-road-trailers-534577/ https://commons.wikimedia.org/wiki/File:Shizuoka_earthquake_struck_room_20090811.jpg https://www.maxpixel.net/Wall-Crack-House-Old-Plaster-353218 https://commons.wikimedia.org/wiki/File:2014_South_Napa_quake_-_Stones_Fallen_From_Face_of_Sam_Kee_-_1_(15014707736).jpg https://commons.wikimedia.org/wiki/File:Earthquake_damage_-_roads.jpg https://commons.wikimedia.org/wiki/File:2010_Chile_earthquake_-_Building_destroyed_in_Concepci%C3%B3n.jpg

Emergency decision-making tree

Prior to the event of a tsunami, tropical cyclone, flooding, landslide or earthquake, speak with your family and teacher about your community's evacuation building or safe place.

Discuss how to respond to possible scenarios, and use the decision tree to help you decide the best course of action.

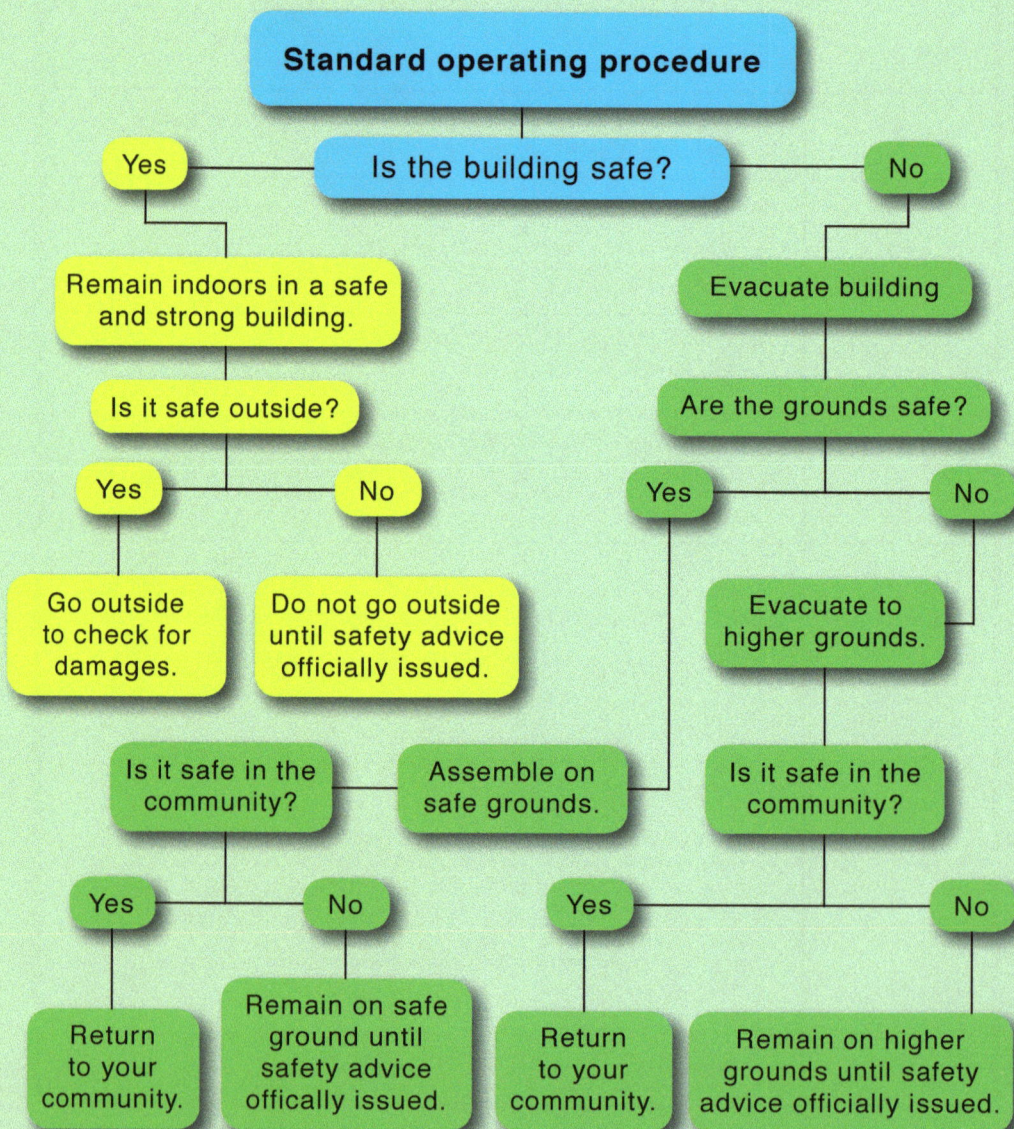

Standard operating procedure

Is the building safe?

Yes → Remain indoors in a safe and strong building.

Is it safe outside?

- Yes → Go outside to check for damages.
- No → Do not go outside until safety advice officially issued.

Is it safe in the community?

- Yes → Return to your community.
- No → Remain on safe ground until safety advice offically issued.

Assemble on safe grounds.

No → Evacuate building

Are the grounds safe?

- Yes → Evacuate to higher grounds.
- No →

Is it safe in the community?

- Yes → Return to your community.
- No → Remain on higher grounds until safety advice officially issued.

Supporting information

Emergency kit

Keep an emergency kit at home for your family.

The kit must contain:

First Aid Kit

Radio

Torch lamp

Batteries

Drinking water

Preserved food

Matches

Use the kit only in case of emergency and replace anything that has been used.

Shelter-in-place

Earthquake:

- Identify safe places where you can protect your head and avoid heavy falling objects.
- Don't forget an earthquake can cause a tsunami.
- If you feel a strong earthquake, go quickly to higher ground, and listen to the radio for warnings.

Tropical cyclone:

- Open louvers on the side of the building, away from wind to reduce the pull force of the wind on the roof.
- Remain calm, stay indoors but clear of doors and windows.
- Remain in the strongest part of the building.

Do not go outside until safety advice is officially issued.

Evacuate building

Assist people with disability and visitors.
Take your emergency kit.
Evacuate to higher ground and move to a safe location.

Tsunami:

- Run to a safe place in high ground or at least 2 km inside the island.
- Wait for at least 2–3 hours after the first wave to return to the village.

Listen to the radio for further information or reach out to the emergency contacts.

You can use these questions to talk about this book with your family, friends and teachers.

What did you learn from this book?

Describe this book in one word. Funny? Scary? Colourful? Interesting?

How did this book make you feel when you finished reading it?

What was your favourite part of this book?

download our reader app
getlibraryforall.org

About the contributors

Library For All works with authors and illustrators from around the world to develop diverse, relevant, high quality stories for young readers. Visit libraryforall.org for the latest news on writers' workshop events, submission guidelines and other creative opportunities.

Did you enjoy this book?

We have hundreds more expertly curated original stories to choose from.

We work in partnership with authors, educators, cultural advisors, governments and NGOs to bring the joy of reading to children everywhere.

Did you know?

We create global impact in these fields by embracing the United Nations Sustainable Development Goals.

libr21.org

www.ingramcontent.com/pod-product-compliance
Lightning Source LLC
Chambersburg PA
CBHW040314050426

42452CB00018B/2834